WHO EATS WHAT?

MOUNTAIN FOOD CHAINS

by Rebecca Pettiford

pogo

Ideas for Parents and Teachers

Pogo Books let children practice reading informational text while introducing them to nonfiction features such as headings, labels, sidebars, maps, and diagrams, as well as a table of contents, glossary, and index.

Carefully leveled text with a strong photo match offers early fluent readers the support they need to succeed.

Before Reading

- "Walk" through the book and point out the various nonfiction features. Ask the student what purpose each feature serves.
- Look at the glossary together. Read and discuss the words.

Read the Book

- Have the child read the book independently.
- Invite him or her to list questions that arise from reading.

After Reading

- Discuss the child's questions. Talk about how he or she might find answers to those questions.
- Prompt the child to think more. Ask: What other mountain animals and plants do you know about? What food chains do you think they are a part of?

Pogo Books are published by Jump!
5357 Penn Avenue South
Minneapolis, MN 55419
www.jumplibrary.com

Library of Congress Cataloging-in-Publication Data

Names: Pettiford, Rebecca, author.
Pettiford, Rebecca. Who eats what?
Title: Mountain food chains / by Rebecca Pettiford.
Description: Minneapolis, MN: Jump!, Inc. [2017]
Series: Who eats what? | Audience: Ages 7-10.
Includes bibliographical references and index.
Identifiers: LCCN 2016031977 (print)
LCCN 2016033070 (ebook)
ISBN 9781620315767 (hardcover: alk. paper)
ISBN 9781620316153 (pbk.)
ISBN 9781624965241 (ebook)
Subjects: LCSH: Mountain ecology–Juvenile literature.
Food chains (Ecology)–Juvenile literature.
Mountain animals–Juvenile literature.
Adaptation (Biology)–Juvenile literature.
Classification: LCC QH541.5.M65 P48 2017 (print)
LCC QH541.5.M65 (ebook) | DDC 577.5/3–dc23
LC record available at https://lccn.loc.gov/2016031977

Editor: Jenny Fretland VanVoorst
Book Designer: Michelle Sonnek
Photo Researcher: Michelle Sonnek

Photo Credits: All photos by Shutterstock except:
age fotostock, 14-15, 19, 20-21bm; Alamy, 1, 12-13, 18; Animals Animals 20-21b; SuperStock, 11.

Printed in the United States of America at Corporate Graphics in North Mankato, Minnesota.

TABLE OF CONTENTS

CHAPTER 1

MOUNTAIN ADAPTATIONS

There are mountains and mountain **ranges** all over the world. This **environment** covers about 20 percent of Earth's surface.

Mountains contain a variety of **ecosystems**. But they have one thing in common. Over short distances, they show big changes in weather and plant and animal life.

At a mountain's higher **elevations**, the air is thin. It is harder to breathe. It is cold and windy. Trees do not grow.

The point at which trees stop growing is called the **timberline**. Some plants can grow above the timberline. They include grasses and **lichens**.

WHERE ARE THEY?

Mountains are found in almost every part of the world. Here are 10 of the longest ranges.

❶ = Andes

❷ = Rocky Mountains

❸ = Great Dividing Range

❹ = Transantarctic

❺ = Brazilian East Coast Range

❻ = Himalayas

❼ = Sumatran/Javan Range

❽ = Tien Shan

❾ = Eastern Ghats

❿ = Altai

Animals that live at higher elevations have **adaptations**. They help animals handle their surroundings. Thick fur keeps them warm. **Hooves** help them climb and hold on to rocks.

CHAPTER 2

THE MOUNTAIN FOOD CHAIN

Like all living things, mountain plants and animals need energy to grow and move. Food is energy. Plants make food from the sun, soil, and water. Animals eat plants and other animals.

A **food chain** shows how energy moves from plants to animals. Each living link in the chain eats the one before it.

marmot
(consumer)

flowers
(producers)

In the mountains, trees, flowers, and shrubs are **producers**. They use energy from the sun, soil, and water to make their own food. They are the first link in the food chain.

Wild goats, elk, and llamas eat plants. So do **ibex** and marmots. They are **consumers**, the next link in the chain.

Animals such as eagles, wolves, and mountain lions are **predators**. They hunt and eat consumers. They are the next link in the food chain.

Large predators will also eat smaller predators. For example, a mountain lion will eat a coyote.

DID YOU KNOW?

Pets can be an easy meal for mountain lions and coyotes. If you live near the mountains, keep a close eye on outdoor pets. Make sure to bring them in at night!

wolf
(predator)

deer
(consumer)

When an animal or plant dies, flies, worms, and **bacteria** break down its body. They are **decomposers**, the last link in the chain.

Decomposers return **nutrients** to the soil. This helps trees and other plants grow.

TAKE A LOOK!

One mountain food chain might look something like this:

Producer: Grass

Predator: Gray Wolf

Consumer: Elk

Decomposer: Bacteria

CHAPTER 3

FOOD CHAIN CLOSE-UPS

Let's look at a simple food chain. Grass grows on the mountain. A hare eats the grass.

An eagle eats the hare. When the eagle dies, bacteria break down its body. The nutrients make the soil rich. New grass grows. The food chain begins again.

Let's look at another food chain.

1) This one starts with flowers.

2) A mountain goat eats the flowers.

3) A mountain lion eats the goat.

4) In time, the mountain lion dies. Worms break down its body.

The nutrients help plants grow. The food chain continues!

TRY THIS!

MOUNTAIN GORILLA FOOD CHAIN

In this book, you explored several mountain food chains. You saw pictures of consumers with hooves. But high in the mountains of central Africa, there is a consumer that looks more like you. It is the mountain gorilla. Use the Internet to look up pictures and information about the mountain gorilla. Ask an adult for help if you need it. Get some paper and a pen. Answer the following questions:

1. In what ways do you look like a mountain gorilla?

2. What producers (plants) does a mountain gorilla eat?

3. What are a mountain gorilla's main predators?

4. What decomposers live in the gorilla's mountain home?

5. Draw a picture of a mountain gorilla. Draw a line to connect it to its food. Add links to the food chain by adding predators. Add decomposers.

GLOSSARY

adaptations: Changes that help plants and animals survive the conditions of a natural area.

bacteria: Tiny life forms that break down dead animals.

consumers: Animals that eat plants.

decomposers: Life forms that break down dead matter.

ecosystems: Ecological communities of living things interacting with their environment.

elevations: Heights.

environment: The whole complex of factors (such as soil, climate, and living things) that influence the form and the ability to survive of a plant or animal or ecological community.

food chain: An ordering of plants and animals in which each uses or eats the one before it for energy.

hooves: Coverings of horn that protect the front of or enclose the ends of the toes of some mammals and that correspond to nails or claws.

ibex: Wild goats with long, curved horns that live in the mountains of Europe, Asia, and North Africa.

lichens: Small plants that grow on rocks and trees.

nutrients: Things, such as proteins, minerals, and vitamins, that people, animals, and plants need to stay strong and healthy.

predators: Animals that hunt and eat other animals.

producers: Plants that make their own food from the sun.

ranges: Groups of mountains.

timberline: An invisible line on a mountain that marks the point above which trees do not grow.

INDEX

TO LEARN MORE

Learning more is as easy as 1, 2, 3.

1) Go to www.factsurfer.com

2) Enter "mountainfoodchains" into the search box.

3) Click the "Surf" button to see a list of websites.

With factsurfer, finding more information is just a click away.